OCEANS ALIVE

Whales

by Ann Herriges

BLASTOFF!
2
READERS

BELLWETHER MEDIA · MINNEAPOLIS, MN

JUL 17 2007

Note to Librarians, Teachers, and Parents:

Blastoff! Readers are carefully developed by literacy experts and combine standards-based content with developmentally appropriate text.

Level 1 provides the most support through repetition of high-frequency words, light text, predictable sentence patterns, and strong visual support.

Level 2 offers early readers a bit more challenge through varied simple sentences, increased text load, and less repetition of high-frequency words.

Level 3 advances early-fluent readers toward fluency through increased text and concept load, less reliance on visuals, longer sentences, and more literary language.

Whichever book is right for your reader, Blastoff! Readers are the perfect books to build confidence and encourage a love of reading that will last a lifetime!

This edition first published in 2007 by Bellwether Media.

No part of this publication may be reproduced in whole or in part without written permission of the publisher. For information regarding permission, write to Bellwether Media Inc., Attention: Permissions Department, Post Office Box 1C, Minnetonka, MN 55345-9998.

Library of Congress Cataloging-in-Publication Data
Herriges, Ann.
  Whales / by Ann Herriges.
    p. cm. — (Blastoff! readers) (Oceans alive!)
Summary: "Simple text and supportive images introduce beginning readers to whales. Intended for students in kindergarten through third grade."
  Includes bibliographical references and index.
  ISBN-10: 1-60014-023-8 (hardcover : alk. paper)
  ISBN-13: 978-1-60014-023-5 (hardcover : alk. paper)
  1. Whales—Juvenile literature. I. Title. II. Series. III. Series: Oceans alive!

QL737.C4H365 2007
599.5—dc22   2006005364

Text copyright © 2007 by Bellwether Media.
Printed in the United States of America.

Table of Contents

Whales are huge **mammals**.

Whales swim in oceans all over the world.

Some whales are the size of
a car. Most are much bigger.

The blue whale is the largest animal that has ever lived. It is the size of a jet airplane.

A whale moves its tail up and down to swim.

Whale tails have two fins
called **flukes**.

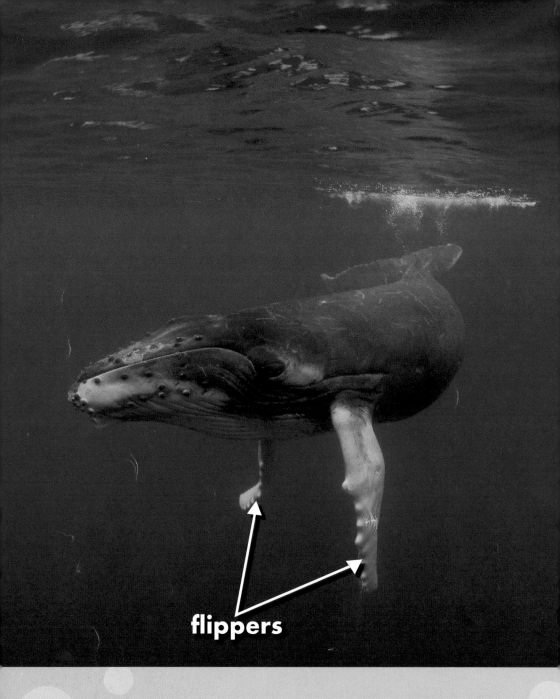

flippers

Whales have two **flippers**. Flippers help whales turn and stop.

10

Whales **breach**. They jump out of the water and land with a big splash!

Whales have smooth skin. It helps them slide through the water.

Whales have **blubber** under their skin. This fat keeps them warm.

13

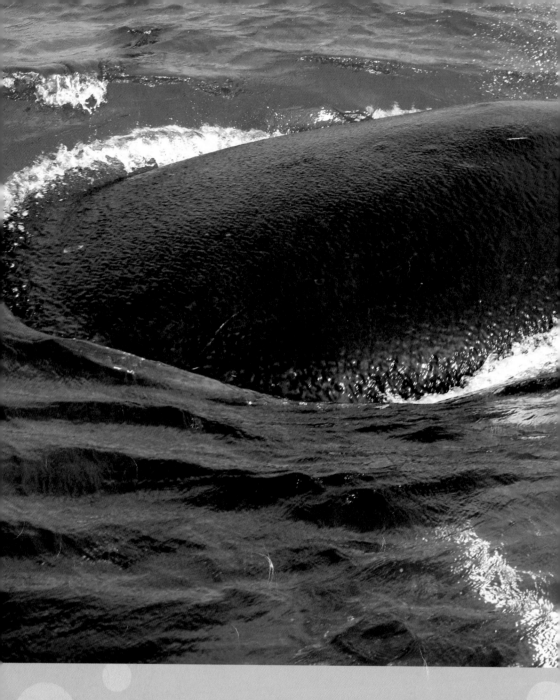

Whales have one or two **blowholes**. They use their blowholes to breathe air.

Whales blow a **spout** into the
air when they breathe out.

Whales groan and sing to talk to each other.

Some whales have sharp teeth. They use their teeth to grab fish and other food.

Some whales have **baleen** instead of teeth. Baleen is like a big net.

baleen

Whales push water through their baleen. The baleen traps food for the whale to eat.

19

Most whales live in groups.
Some whales **migrate**.

They swim to warm waters in autumn and back to cool waters in the spring.

Glossary

baleen—thin plates that hang from the top of a whale's mouth; baleen is made of the same material as your fingernails.

blowhole—a breathing hole at the top of an ocean mammal's head; whales with teeth have one blowhole and whales with baleen have two blowholes.

blubber—a thick layer of fat just under the skin; whales that live in colder waters have thicker blubber than whales that live in warm waters.

breach—to jump out of the water and land hard with a splash; some scientists think the sound of the splash is a message to other whales.

flipper—a wide, flat limb that some ocean animals use to swim

flukes—the two fins at the end of a whale's tail

mammal—an animal with a backbone that is warm-blooded and has hair; mammals are born alive and drink their mother's milk.

migrate—to move from one place to another; some whales migrate to colder waters in the spring to find food.

spout—a cloud of misty water that whales spray when they breathe out a blowhole

To Learn More

AT THE LIBRARY

Davies, Nicola. *Big Blue Whale*. Cambridge, Mass.: Candlewick Press, 1997.

Donaldson, Julia. *The Snail and the Whale*. New York: Dial Books for Young Readers, 2004.

Gibbons, Gail. *Whales*. New York: Holiday House, 1991.

James, Simon. *Dear Mr. Blueberry*. New York: M.K. McElderry Books, 1991.

Tokuda, Wendy, and Richard Hall. *Humphrey the Lost Whale*. Union City, Calif.: Heian, 1986.

Van Dusen, Chris. *Down to the Sea with Mr. Magee*. San Francisco, Calif.: Chronicle Books, 2000.

ON THE WEB

Learning more about whales is as easy as 1, 2, 3.

1. Go to www.factsurfer.com

2. Enter "whales" into search box.

3. Click the "Surf" button and you will see a list of related web sites.

With factsurfer.com, finding more information is just a click away.

Index